This book belongs to:

....

Mrs Wordsmith®

GET READING WITH

PHONICS

Bearnice

Bogart

Brick

Plato

Grit

Yin & Yang

Armie

Stax

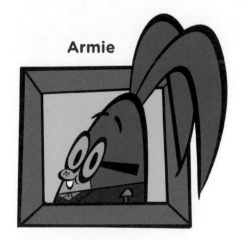

Oz

MEET THE
CHARACTERS

Scan the QR code

CONTENTS

Mrs Wordsmith Get Reading with Phonics
is divided into eight easy-to-follow sections
containing 51 phoneme–grapheme correspondences
in the order they are taught in schools.
It is designed for kids in kindergarten.

What is in this book?

Phonics is all about linking sounds (phonemes) to the letters (graphemes) that represent them in writing, so it is an important first step when learning to read. In this book, kids will learn to recognize new graphemes and decode new words alongside engaging illustrations and sentences that put those words in context. This ensures that kids practice using their new skills in a meaningful and memorable way.

Phonics for Grown-Ups

Helping kids with phonics can be a daunting task. There are a few technical terms that you need to know and some basic ideas that will make the whole process a lot easier.

To guarantee success using this book (and to turn you into an expert), we've included a short, easy-to-follow guide for adults that covers all things phonics. Turn to page 11 for all the information you need to support your little reader on their journey.

The most important thing when learning phonics is that you cover the content in the correct order. Each piece of new learning builds on the last, so start from the beginning and work your way through the chapters.

Chapters 1–8

In Chapters 1 and 2, kids will learn simple phoneme–grapheme correspondences like **s**, **a**, **t**, **p**, **m**, **d**, and **o**, as well as how to decode (read) three-letter words using the letters that they have already learned.

In Chapters 3 and 4, kids will learn phoneme–grapheme correspondences for more consonants like **r**, **h**, **b**, **j**, **v**, and **w**, as well as the consonant teams **ff**, **ll**, and **ss**. These consonant teams still represent a single sound despite consisting of two letters.

In Chapters 5 and 6, kids will learn consonant teams like **qu**, **ch**, and **sh**, two-letter vowel teams like **ai**, **ee**, and **oa**, and the three-letter vowel team **igh** as in *light*.

In Chapters 7 and 8, kids will learn more two-letter vowel teams like **ar**, **or**, and **ur** and three-letter vowel teams like **ear**, **air**, and **ire**.

How do I use this book?

Learning Pages

Each section begins with a series of learning pages that introduce the new phoneme-grapheme correspondences.

Scan the QR code

Scan the QR code with your device and listen to how the phoneme (sound) is pronounced.

2

Repeat the sound several times with your child while looking at the grapheme (letter or group of letters). Read the main word aloud and emphasize where the phoneme is placed.

3

Read this sentence aloud to your child, emphasizing the targeted phoneme and putting the new word in context.

4

Trace the letter

Encourage your child to trace the letter with their finger, helping them start at the right point and lift their finger off the page where necessary. Then try tracing it with a pencil. Finally, encourage them to try to write it.

5

Read the extra words to your child, emphasizing the targeted phoneme as you do and then discuss what they mean.

Activity Pages

After the learning pages, you will get to a set of activity pages focused around the same phoneme–grapheme correspondences. These provide practice and context, as well as developing text comprehension.

Many of the activity pages in this book are designed to be used with stickers. You will find all the stickers that you need at the back of the book. Show your child how to find a sticker and stick it in the allocated place on the page.

The process of peeling and placing stickers is great for their fine motor skills.

Encourage your child to experiment with the stickers. There's no need to panic if you stick something in the wrong place. The stickers can be peeled off and restuck a few times.

Tip!

If it helps, cut out the sticker pages at the back of the book so that you don't have to flip back and forth.

Practicing High-Frequency Words

In order to be able to read sentences with speed and fluency, which is the ultimate goal of learning phonics, kids also need to learn some high-frequency words.

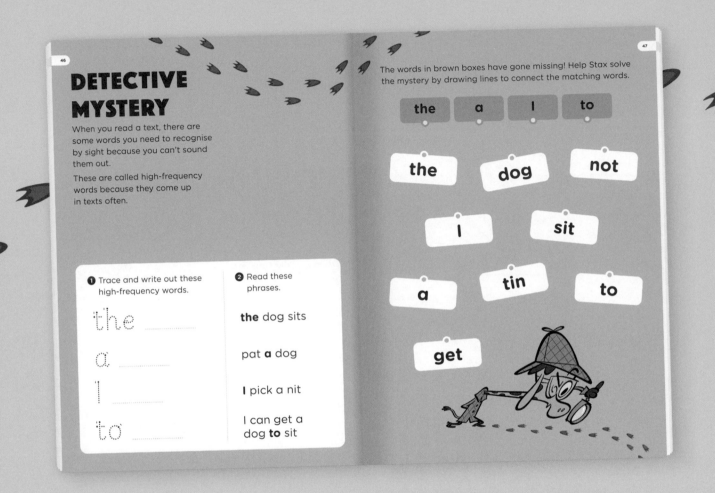

Pages 46, 82, and 138 introduce some very common words that are important for kids to be able to identify **by sight**. They include some tricky words with irregular spellings that make them difficult to master with phonics alone.

When kids are learning to read, words appearing in different fonts or with capitalization or punctuation can be confusing. For this reason, we've kept the formatting to a minimum by keeping almost all letters in the lower case and avoiding periods.

PHONICS FOR GROWN-UPS

All the **must-know phonics terms** and concepts explained in one handy guide! Read this from start to finish for a crash course or use it as a reference tool whenever you need a reminder.

What is a phoneme?

A phoneme is the smallest unit of sound. It is the sound associated with a letter or group of letters. Each sound in a word is a phoneme. For example, the letter **t** makes the sound **/t/** as in *tap*. Phonemes are often represented by more than one grapheme (a letter or a combination of letters). For example, the phoneme **/f/** can be written **f** as in *funny*, **ff** as in *bluff*, **ph** as in *phone*, or even **gh** as in *laugh*.

How many phonemes are there?

There are 44 phonemes (sounds) in the English language. This means that all words in spoken English are made from a combination of these 44 individual phonemes.

What is a grapheme?

A grapheme is a letter or group of letters that is used to represent a phoneme (sound) on the page. In other words, a grapheme is the written form of a sound. For example, the word *tap* consists of the three graphemes **t**, **a**, and **p**. A grapheme can consist of more than one letter; for example, **tch** in *catch* is a single grapheme because it corresponds to a single sound.

At the same time, a grapheme (letter or group of letters) can represent more than one phoneme (sound). For example, the letter **g** has a soft sound (as in *giraffe*) and hard sound (as in *get*). In these two words, the letter **g** is pronounced differently.

How many graphemes are there?

There are around 250 graphemes in English. This is because most phonemes have more than one grapheme corresponding to them. For example, the phoneme **/f/** has four graphemes: **f**, **ff**, **ph**, and **gh**.

What is phonics?

Because English consists of 44 phonemes (sounds) but around 250 graphemes (different written representations for these sounds), it does not have a strict one-to-one correspondence between letters and sounds. But this doesn't mean that English is entirely irregular. It still has numerous regular patterns. Phonics is the method that helps kids become aware of these regularities. In other words, phonics helps them learn the most common sounds that correspond to each grapheme, which in turn enables them to read!

What is phonological awareness?

Phonological awareness is the awareness of sounds in spoken words, as well as the ability to manipulate those sounds. Phonological awareness is an umbrella term for basic skills like being able to identify the number of words in a sentence, the syllables within a word and words that rhyme, as well as more advanced skills like identifying individual phonemes in each word.

What is phonemic awareness?

Phonemic awareness is the most advanced level of phonological awareness. It refers to the ability to focus on individual sounds (phonemes) in spoken words: to break them apart; to put them back together; and to swap one for another to make new words. The ability to hear and differentiate individual sounds underpins all phonics learning and must come first.

What are blending and segmenting?

One of the key ways to develop phonemic awareness is through blending and segmenting words. The process of segmenting involves breaking words down into individual sounds, like breaking down the word *cat* into its individual phonemes **/c/**, **/a/**, **/t/** and saying these sounds aloud. The process of blending involves putting phonemes together to make up words, like understanding that you can put together the sounds **/c/**, **/a/**, **/t/** to make the word *cat* if you pronounce them quickly one after another. Practicing blending and segmenting is a critical building block of phonics, early reading and writing.

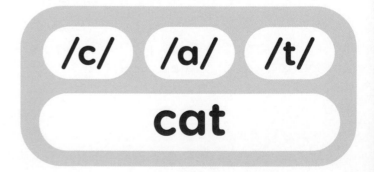

What are decoding and encoding?

Decoding involves translating printed words to sounds. It is the process of reading words in text. When a child reads the words **the ball is big**, they need to understand what the letters are, what sound each letter makes, and how the letters blend together to create words.

Encoding is the opposite of decoding. It is the process of using individual sounds and letters to build and write words. In this sense, decoding is more relevant to reading and encoding is more relevant to spelling. Both processes require an understanding of what the individual sounds (phonemes) in a word are.

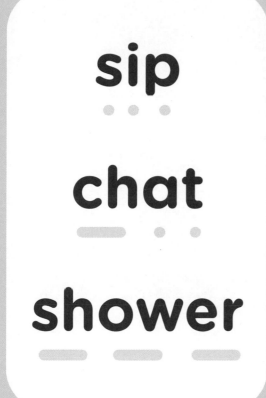

What are consonant teams and vowel teams?

Consonant teams and vowel teams can be a combination of two or three letters representing one sound. For example, **s** and **h** together make **sh** as in *shop*, while **i**, **g**, and **h** together make **igh** as in *sigh*.

Kids often need help spotting when a word has a consonant team or vowel team. One method for this is drawing a dot under a single letter that makes a single sound and drawing a line under a consonant team or vowel team. This method is called **sound buttoning**, and you can find some practice activities for it on page 26 and page 64.

What are CVC words?

CVC words consist of three sounds that follow a consonant/vowel/consonant pattern. These words are considered the simplest words for emerging readers to decode by blending the three sounds together. For example:

 **CVC**   **cat**   **cup**   **log**   **shop**   **fuss**

LET'S DO THIS!

Now that all that grown-up stuff is out of the way,
let's get reading! Turn the page to join our mischievous
characters as they take you on a hilarious reading adventure.

Bearnice **sat** on Bogart.

s

1. Sound out the word and then blend the sounds together.

sat

2. Trace the dotted grapheme with your finger.

sat

3. Write the grapheme.

Other words with the **s** sound:
sit **sip**

a

1 Sound out the word and then blend the sounds together.

pat

2 Trace the dotted grapheme with your finger.

pat

3 Write the grapheme.

a

Other words with the **a** sound:
at
pan

Bearnice gave Grit a **pat** on the head.

Bogart lived in
an anchovy **tin**.

t

1 Sound out
the word and
then blend the
sounds together.

tin

2 Trace the dotted
grapheme with
your finger.

 in

3 Write the
grapheme.

Other words
with the
t sound:

tan

tip

p

1 Sound out the word and then blend the sounds together.

tap

2 Trace the dotted grapheme with your finger.

tap

3 Write the grapheme.

p

Other words with the **p** sound:

pit

nip

Bearnice gave the screen a little **tap**.

Oz took a **sip** of tea.

i

1. Sound out the word and then blend the sounds together.

sip

2. Trace the dotted grapheme with your finger.

s i p

3. Write the grapheme.

Other words with the **i** sound:

it

pit

n

1. Sound out the word and then blend the sounds together.

nap

2. Trace the dotted grapheme with your finger.

ⁿap

3. Write the grapheme.

ⁿ

Other words with the **n** sound:
nit
pin

Brick had a **nap**.

SPACE SURFING

Stax was surfing through space when he stumbled across a new galaxy!

Use the moon stickers to write six words with **a** in the middle, like **c-a-t**.

Add sticker here.

Add sticker here.

Add sticker here.

Add sticker here.

Add sticker here.

Add sticker here.

Turn to page 150 for stickers.

Add sticker here.

a

Add sticker here.

Add sticker here.

a

Add sticker here.

Add sticker here.

a

Add sticker here.

BUBBLE BATH

Learning words in the bathtub can be tricky, especially when the letters start floating away! Can you help Yin and Yang complete these words?

Use the bubble stickers to write six words with **i** in the middle, like **k-i-t**.

Add sticker here.

i

Add sticker here.

Add sticker here.

i

Add sticker here.

Add sticker here.

i

Add sticker here.

Turn to pages 150 and 151 for stickers.

Add sticker here.

i

Add sticker here.

Add sticker here.

i

Add sticker here.

Add sticker here.

i

Add sticker here.

SOUND BUTTONS

Sound buttons are visual cues that help you identify when a single letter makes a single sound versus when a combination of letters makes a single sound. This method helps you decode words by segmenting them into graphemes.

Step 1:
When a single letter makes
one sound, put a dot under it.

Step 2:
Blend and read the words.

Now it's your turn! Sound button the words below.
Then blend and read the words.

sip

nap

pan

tan

tap

sap

sat

SPOT THE ALIENS

Armie is on a space mission to learn as many words as he can. Wait a minute ... Some of these words are aliens! Alien words don't mean anything! Can you help Armie find the real words?

Read each word carefully to help you decide if it is real or alien. Put a **star sticker** under the real words and an **alien sticker** under the alien words.

Remember, you can add sound buttons to help you read the words.

sit

Add sticker here.

tas

Add sticker here.

Turn to page 151 for stickers.

sip

Add sticker here.

tap

Add sticker here.

nit

Add sticker here.

san

Add sticker here.

nas

Add sticker here.

pit

Add sticker here.

Now you can read ...
Pit, **pat**, **pin** and **tin**, **tan**, **tip**.
Nap, **nip**, **nit** and **sip**, **sat**, **sit**.

sat on
a pin

nap in a
tin can

The best **map**
is a treasure **map**.

m

1. Sound out the word and then blend the sounds together.

map

2. Trace the dotted grapheme with your finger.

 ap

3. Write the grapheme.

Other words with the **m** sound:

man

mat

d

1 Sound out the word and then blend the sounds together.

sad

2 Trace the dotted grapheme with your finger.

sad

3 Write the grapheme.

d

Other words with the **d** sound:
dim **pad**

Yin and Yang felt **sad**.

"May I have this dance?" Plato asked his **mop**.

o

1) Sound out the word and then blend the sounds together.

mop

2 Trace the dotted grapheme with your finger.

m·o·p

Write the grapheme.

Other words with the **o** sound:

on

top

pot

g

1. Sound out the word and then blend the sounds together.

dig

2. Trace the dotted grapheme with your finger.

dig

3. Write the grapheme.

g

Other words with the **g** sound:

gas

dog

tag

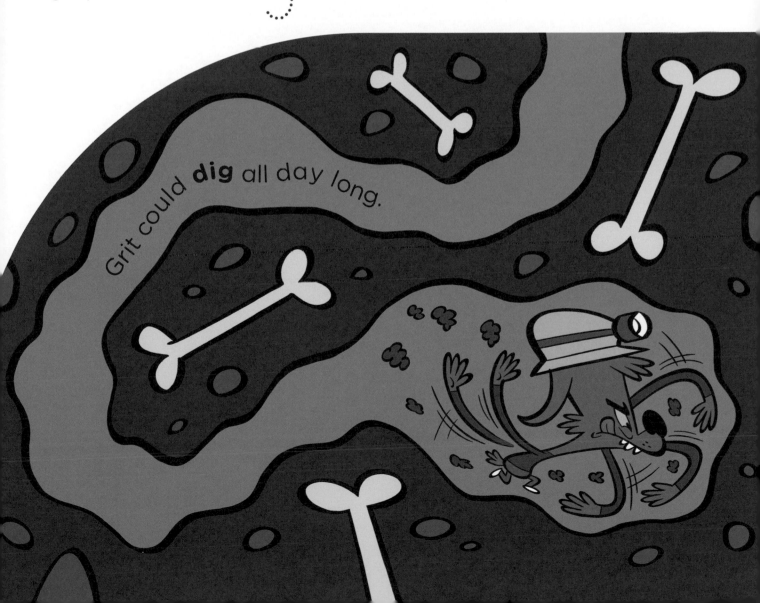

Grit could **dig** all day long.

Yin's **cap** was a little too big.

c

① Sound out the word and then blend the sounds together.

cap

② Trace the dotted grapheme with your finger.

cap

Write the grapheme.

c

Other words with **c**:

can

cat

cot

k

1 Sound out the word and then blend the sounds together.

kit

2 Trace the dotted grapheme with your finger.

kit

3 Write the grapheme.

k

Other words with the **k** sound:

kin

kid

Oz opened her **kit**.

Bogart was inside a **sock**.

ck

1. Sound out the word and then blend the sounds together.

sock

2. Trace the dotted grapheme with your finger.

so

3. Write the grapheme.

Other words with **ck**:

kick

pick

tick

e

1. Sound out the word and then blend the sounds together.

pet

2. Trace the dotted grapheme with your finger.

pet

3. Write the grapheme.

e

Other words with the **e** sound:

net

ten

get

Bearnice loves her **pet**.

SCRUB UP!

There are bubbles everywhere!
Can you help Stax complete these
words before the letters float away?

Use the bubble stickers
to write six words with
o in the middle,
like **p-o-t**.

Add sticker here.

O

Add sticker here.

Add sticker here.

O

Add sticker here.

Add sticker here.

Add sticker here.

Add sticker here.

Add sticker here.

Add sticker here.

Add sticker here.

Add sticker here.

Add sticker here.

Turn to page 154 for stickers.

PLATO'S BIRTHDAY

It's the thought that counts! Help Plato unwrap his strange collection of birthday presents.

Circle the word that matches each gift.

1

pig

~~dog~~ (dog circled)

2

cat

pan

3

kit

pen

5

mop

top

4

not

pig

6

met

net

8

sick

sack

7

sock

kick

STARGAZING

Armie was stargazing when he stumbled across another new galaxy!

Use the planet stickers to write six words with **e** in the middle, like **l-e-g**.

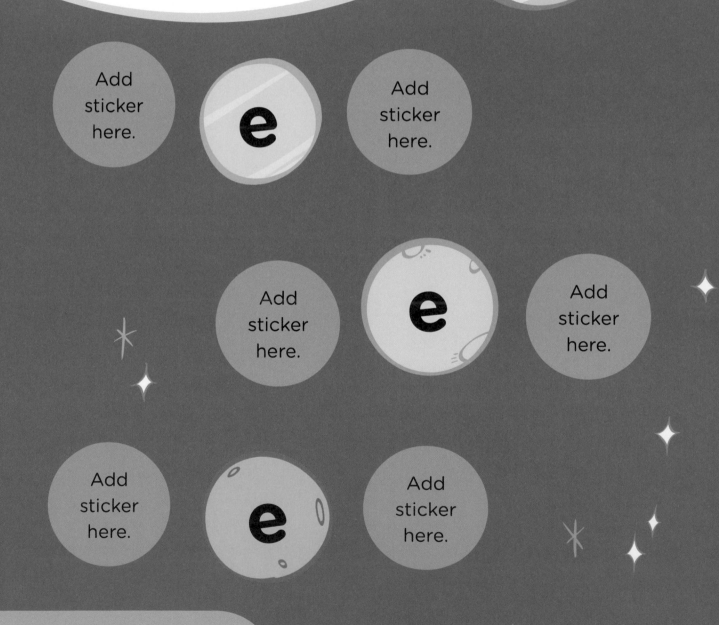

Add sticker here.

e

Add sticker here.

Add sticker here.

e

Add sticker here.

Add sticker here.

e

Add sticker here.

Turn to pages 154 and 155 for stickers.

DETECTIVE MYSTERY

When you read a text, there are some words you need to recognize by sight because you can't sound them out.

These are called high-frequency words because they come up in texts often.

1 Trace and write out these high-frequency words.

the _____

a _____

i _____

to _____

2 Read these phrases.

the dog sits

pat **a** dog

I pick a nit

I can get a dog **to** sit

Stax needs to find the words in the brown boxes. Help him solve the mystery by drawing lines to connect the matching words.

SCRAPBOOK!

Yin and Grit are scrapbooking!
Help them match the captions to the pictures.

Read each phrase and stick the matching picture sticker above it.

Add sticker here.

I nap

Add sticker here.

the cat

I am sick

Turn to pages 155 and 158 for stickers.

Add
sticker
here.

a stick

Add
sticker
here.

a snack

Add
sticker
here.

the pig

Add
sticker
here.

the sad dog

Add
sticker
here.

to the top

Look what you've done!
You've learned six new sounds,
And each new one
Unlocks even more fun.

a pig map

a pet
sock

a dog cap

Not just **map**, **mat**, and **mad**,
But **dog**, **dig**, and **dad**,
Cap, **kit**, and **sock**,
And **pet**, **pig**, and **pad**.

Yin and Yang jumped in **mud**.

u

1. Sound out the word and then blend the sounds together.

mud

2. Trace the dotted grapheme with your finger.

mud

3. Write the grapheme.

Other words with the **u** sound:

cut

nut

sun

r

1 Sound out the word and then blend the sounds together.

run

2 Trace the dotted grapheme with your finger.

run

3 Write the grapheme.

r

Other words with the **r** sound:

red

rat

rock

Run, Stax, **run!**

The twins gave
Brick a big **hug**.

h

1. Sound out the word and then blend the sounds together.

hug

2. Trace the dotted grapheme with your finger.

ug

3. Write the grapheme.

h

Other words with the **h** sound:

hat

hit

him

b

1) Sound out the word and then blend the sounds together.

bed

2 Trace the dotted grapheme with your finger.

bed

3 Write the grapheme.

b

Other words with the **b** sound:

rub

bad

big

Grit lay in **bed** all morning.

Brick is Plato's biggest **fan**.

f

1) Sound out the word and then blend the sounds together.

fan

2) Trace the dotted grapheme with your finger.

fan

3) Write the grapheme.

f

Other words with the **f** sound:

fit

fed

fun

ff

1 Sound out the word and then blend the sounds together.

puff

2 Trace the dotted grapheme with your finger.

puff

3 Write the grapheme.

ff

Other words with **ff**:
off
huff
sniff

Stax blew out the candles in one **puff**.

Armie, Bearnice, and Stax ran along a **log**.

l

1 Sound out the word and then blend the sounds together.

log

2 Trace the dotted grapheme with your finger.

og

3 Write the grapheme.

Other words with the **l** sound:

lip

lot

leg

ll

1 Sound out the word and then blend the sounds together.

hill

2 Trace the dotted grapheme with your finger.

hill

3 Write the grapheme.

Other words with **ll**:

tell

bell

fell

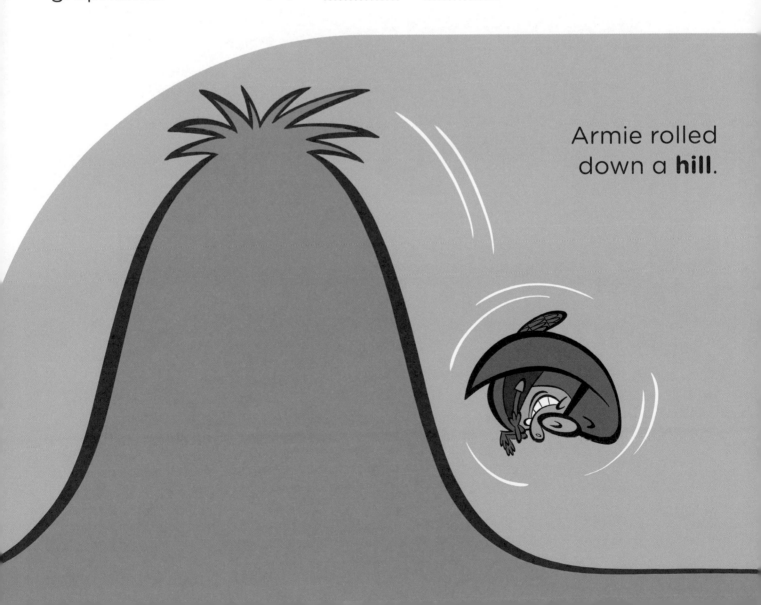

Armie rolled down a **hill**.

Grit's bedroom is a **mess**.

ss

1. Sound out the word and then blend the sounds together.

mess

2. Trace the dotted grapheme with your finger.

mess

Write the grapheme.

ss

Other words with **ss**:

kiss

less

boss

cleaning
in progre**ss**

please turn
the page

PLANET HOPPING

Stax was planet hopping when he stumbled across yet another new galaxy!

Use the planet and moon stickers to write six words with **u** in the middle, like **s-u-n**.

Add sticker here.

u

Add sticker here.

Add sticker here.

u

Add sticker here.

Turn to pages 159 and 162 for stickers.

Add sticker here.

Add sticker here.

Add sticker here.

Add sticker here.

Add sticker here.

Add sticker here.

Add sticker here.

Add sticker here.

SOUND BUTTONS

Sound buttons are visual cues that help you identify when a single letter makes a single sound versus when a combination of letters makes a single sound. This method helps you decode words by segmenting them into graphemes.

Step 1:
When a single letter makes
one sound, put a dot under it.

big

When a combination of letters (a consonant team or vowel team) makes one sound, underline them.

luck

Step 2:
Blend and read the words.

Now it's your turn! Sound button the words below.
Then blend and read the words.

fill

fog

miss

duck

tell

bill

bun

sniff

BUBBLEGUM

Oz is blowing bubblegum in class!
What can you see inside Oz's
bubbles? Circle the word
that matches what
is in each bubble.

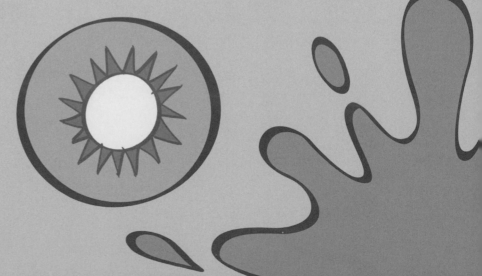

1

bed
bin

2

sun
fun

3

bit
bat

4

puff
bell

5

run
rat

6

kiss
less

7

hot
had

8

cliff
sniff

BEACH DAY

Is that Brick over there, buried in the sand?
What other buried treasures can you see?
Use stickers to complete the words.

1   b a   Add sticker here.

2   Add sticker here.   a t

3   Add sticker here.   o g

Turn to page 162 for stickers.

4 b Add sticker here. **g**

5 d o Add sticker here.

6 Add sticker here. u s

Six more sounds. Whoa! Look at you!
That's too many words for us to run through!

a mud bed

a fog kiss

Not just **rug**, **mug**, and **bus**, but **miss**, **less**, and **kiss**.
You know words like **mud**, and **mull**, and **muck**,
Like **bell**, **bed**, and **boss**, and **pug**, **hub**, and **hug**!
You know **bug** and **puff**, and **fog** and **luck**.
You know **tick** and **tock**, and **pick** and **puck**.

That's too much **jam**, Oz!

j

1 Sound out the word and then blend the sounds together.

jam

2 Trace the dotted grapheme with your finger.

jam

3 Write the grapheme.

Other words with the **j** sound:

jog

jet

▶ Sound out the word and then blend the sounds together.

van

▶ Trace the dotted grapheme with your finger.

v̇an

▶ Write the grapheme.

v̇ ....

Other words with the **v** sound:

vet

vat

Plato drove his **van**.

Grit began to **wag** his tail.

w

1 Sound out the word and then blend the sounds together.

wag

2 Trace the dotted grapheme with your finger.

wag

3 Write the grapheme.

w

Other words with the **w** sound:

wet

web

will

x

1 Sound out the word and then blend the sounds together.

fix

2 Trace the dotted grapheme with your finger.

fix

3 Write the grapheme.

x

Other words with the **x** sound:

box

fox

six

Yin and Yang tried to **fix** the vase.

Yuck! This T-shirt stinks!

y

1. Sound out the word and then blend the sounds together.

yuck

2. Trace the dotted grapheme with your finger.

yuck

3. Write the grapheme.

y

Other words with the **y** sound:

yes

yap

yell

z

1 Sound out the word and then blend the sounds together.

zig-zag

2 Trace the dotted grapheme with your finger.

zig-zag

3 Write the grapheme.

z

Other words with the **z** sound:

zip

zap

"My neck is NOT a **zig-zag**!" said Stax.

TOASTING MARSHMALLOWS

Bogart can't wait to toast these marshmallows! Complete these words using the delicious-looking marshmallow stickers. When you're done, blend the sounds to read each word.

b o

Add sticker here.

Add sticker here.

a m

Turn to pages 162 and 163 for stickers.

Add sticker here.

i

g

Add sticker here.

e

s

Add sticker here.

i

p

Add sticker here.

e

b

s

i

Add sticker here.

DESERT DUNES

Brick is hot and thirsty! Help him find the objects buried in the sand! Complete these words by writing in the missing letters.

1 .... **ig**

2 **fo** ....

3 .... **am**

4 .... **eb**

5 **si** ....

6 **bo** ....

7 .... **ip**

Use these graphemes to help you with the answers.

z   w

x   j

DETECTIVE MYSTERY

When you read a text, there are some words you need to recognize by sight because you can't sound them out.

These are called high-frequency words because they come up in texts often.

1 Trace and write out these high-frequency words.

he

she

is

my

her

2 Read these phrases.

he naps

she runs

she **is** not sad

my dog is big

her cat is not big

Stax needs to find the words in the green boxes. Help him solve the mystery by drawing lines to connect the matching words.

| he | she | is | my | her |

is

wet

cat

nap

she

map

my

run

he

nit

big

her

SCRAPBOOK!

Oz is scrapbooking! Help her match the captions to the pictures.

Read each phrase and stick the matching picture sticker above it.

Add sticker here.

she is sad

Add sticker here.

my bed

Add sticker here.

her pen

Turn to pages 163 and 166 for stickers.

Add sticker here.

my bag is big

he is glad

Add sticker here.

she is in the box

Add sticker here.

her hat is big

Add sticker here.

he sat on the hill

a jam wig

Yeesh! That was quite a wacky set ...
You learned **j** and **v** and **w** and **x**,
But **y** and **z** were the weirdest ones yet!

a yuck mix

There's **jam** and **job**, and **win** and **wig**,
Van and **vat**, and **zig-zag** and **jig**.
You've seen **yuck** and **fix**, and **zit** and **yell**.
You know **web** and **mix** and **well** as well!

a zig -zag well

"**Buzz buzz**,"
went the bees.

zz

1. Sound out the word and then blend the sounds together.

buzz

2. Trace the dotted grapheme with your finger.

buzz

3. Write the grapheme.

zz

Other words with **zz**:

fizz

fuzz

jazz

qu

1 Sound out the word and then blend the sounds together.

quack

2 Trace the dotted grapheme with your finger.

quack

3 Write the grapheme.

qu

Other words with the **qu** sound:

quit

quick

quiz

The ducks were confused when Plato started to **quack**.

Plato called his friend for a nice, long **chat**.

ch

① Sound out the word and then blend the sounds together.

chat

② Trace the dotted grapheme with your finger.

ch at

③ Write the grapheme.

ch

Other words with the **ch** sound:

chip

chin

rich

sh

1 Sound out the word and then blend the sounds together.

ship

2 Trace the dotted grapheme with your finger.

 **ip**

3 Write the grapheme.

Other words with the **sh** sound:
shop
fish
wish

The twins sailed around the world on their **ship**.

What a bright
and beautiful **moth**!

th

1. Sound out the word and then blend the sounds together.

moth

2. Trace the dotted grapheme with your finger.

mo**th**

3. Write the grapheme.

th

Other words with the **th** sound:

thin

thick

cloth

ng

1 Sound out the word and then blend the sounds together.

long

2 Trace the dotted grapheme with your finger.

long

3 Write the grapheme.

ng

Other words with the **ng** sound:

song

king

wing

Stax's hair was very **long**.

SUSHI

Another round of salmon maki for the table, please!

Complete these words using the sushi stickers. When you're done, blend the sounds to read each word.

 **i** **ck**

Add sticker here.

Add sticker here. **i** **ck**

Turn to page 166 for stickers.

Add sticker here.

i **n**

j **a** Add sticker here.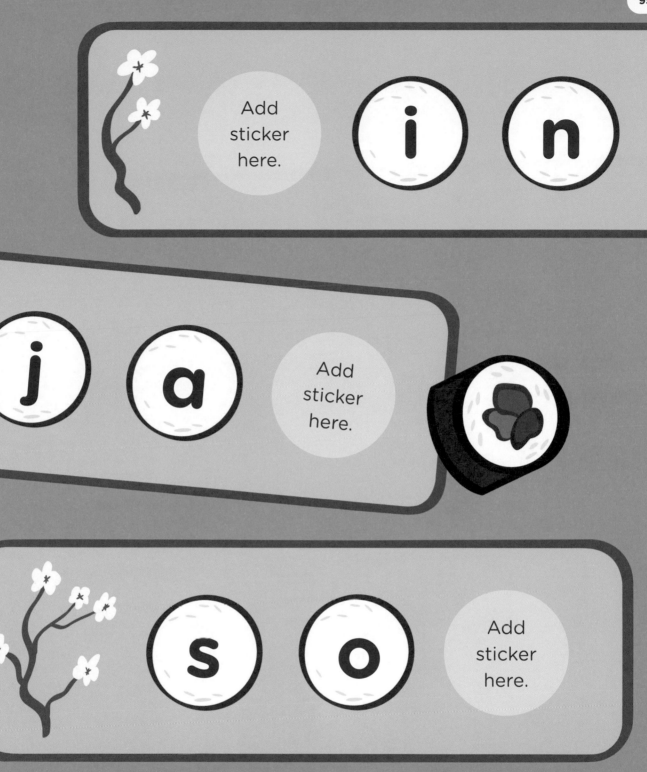

Add sticker here.

s **o** Add sticker here.

Add sticker here.

o

Add sticker here.

OZ'S BIRTHDAY

What do you get the ostrich who has everything? Her guests weren't too sure either. Help Oz unwrap her strange collection of birthday presents.

Circle the word that matches each gift.

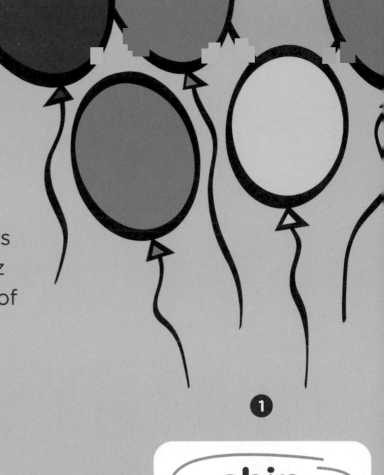

1

ship

rush

2

ring
sing

3

wish
fish

4

thick
moth

5

sell
shell

6

chess
quit

SPOT THE ALIENS

Oh no ... There's been an alien invasion at sea!
Alien words don't mean anything. Can you find the real words?

Read each word carefully to help you decide if it is real or alien.
Put a **dolphin sticker** under the real words and an **alien sticker**
under the alien words.

Remember, you can add sound buttons
to help you read the words.

wung

Add
sticker
here.

quit

Add
sticker
here.

**Turn to page 167
for stickers.**

chiss

Add
sticker
here.

thing

Add
sticker
here.

shop

Add
sticker
here.

kizz

Add
sticker
here.

such

Add
sticker
here.

Watch out—**quick** learner,
Coming through!
A little of **this** and a little of **that**.
How many words have you under your hat?

gush of fuzz

a quack chat

Chat and **chip**, and **chap** and **chop**.
Quit, **quack**, **quiz**, and **ship**, **shut**, **shop**.
Buzz and **fuzz**, and **sing** and **song**,
Gush and **gong**, and **lush** and **long**!

Stax protected Plato from the **rain**.

ai

1. Sound out the word and then blend the sounds together.

rain

2. Trace the dotted grapheme with your finger.

3. Write the grapheme.

Other words with the **ai** sound:

sail

tail

paint

ee

1 Sound out the word and then blend the sounds together.

feel

2 Trace the dotted grapheme with your finger.

feel

3 Write the grapheme.

ee

Other words with the **ee** sound:

bee

need

queen

The movie made Armie **feel** sad.

Bogart did not want to **fight** Brick.

igh

1 Sound out the word and then blend the sounds together.

fight

2 Trace the dotted grapheme with your finger.

fight

3 Write the grapheme.

igh

Other words with the **igh** sound:

right

night

high

oa

1. Sound out the word and then blend the sounds together.

soap

2. Trace the dotted grapheme with your finger.

soap

3. Write the grapheme.

oa _____

Other words with the **oa** sound:

boat

road

coat

Plato washed all over with **soap**.

Bearnice needed a bigger **pool**.

oo

1) Sound out the word and then blend the sounds together.

pool

2) Trace the dotted grapheme with your finger.

pool

3) Write the grapheme.

o o

Other words with the (long) **oo** sound:

too

food

room

oo

1 Sound out the word and then blend the sounds together.

cook

2 Trace the dotted grapheme with your finger.

cook

3 Write the grapheme.

o o

Other words with the (short) **oo** sound:

book

good

took

Grit loved to **cook**.

TOASTING MARSHMALLOWS

Bogart can't wait to toast more marshmallows! Complete these words using the delicious-looking marshmallow stickers. When you're done, blend the sounds to read each word.

n   Add sticker here.   t

n   Add sticker here.   d

Turn to pages 167 and 170 for stickers.

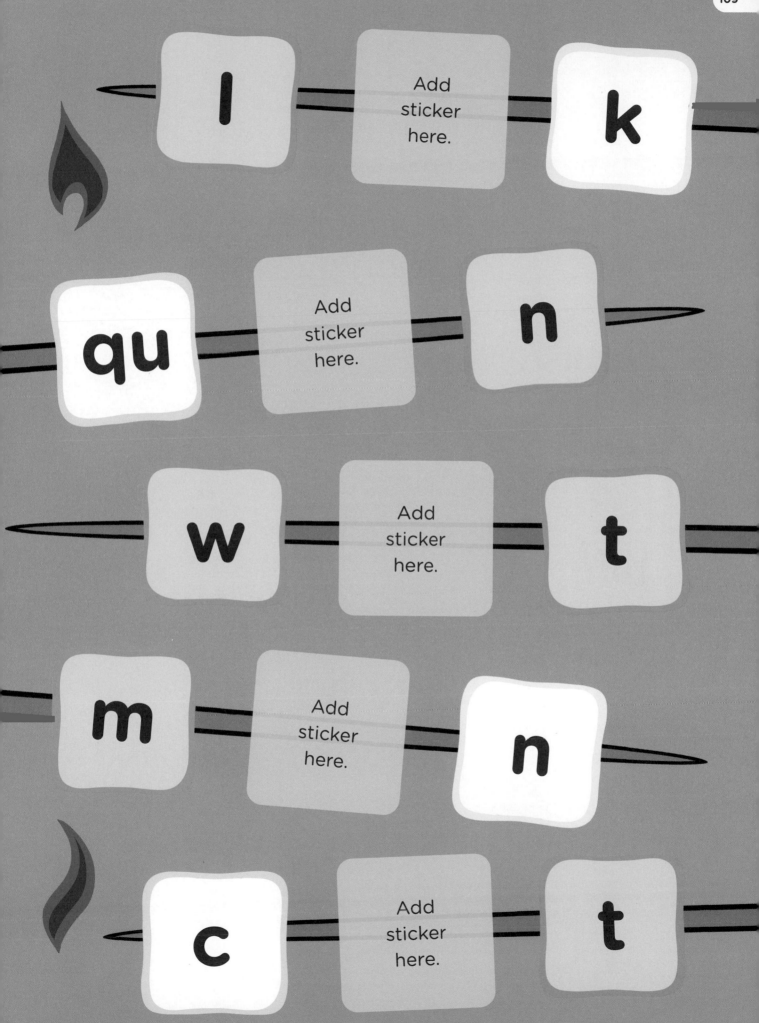

BUBBLEGUM

Bearnice is blowing bubblegum in class! What can you see inside Bearnice's bubbles? Circle the word that matches what is in each bubble.

1

(boat)
foam

2

took
book

3

keep
bee

5

light

right

4

boot

root

6

train

pain

8

cook

wool

7

seed

meet

SNOW DAY

Can you stop throwing snowballs for one minute and help Oz? She's lost some things in the snow!

Complete these words by writing in the missing letters.

❶ c _____ t

❷ r _____ t

❸ t _____ l

5 sh............p

4 n............l

7 sn............l

6 w............d

Use these graphemes to help you with the answers.

oa ee ai

oo igh

Oo! **Igh**! **Ee**! **Ai**!
That's an awful lot
of long sounds
for one day!

soak a tail

a leek rail

There's **sigh** and **high** and **nigh** and **thigh**,
There's **week**, **feel**, **sleep** and **cheek**, **peel**, **leek**.
There's **paint**, **boat**, **sail** and **pain**, **coat**, **mail**.
There's **rail** and **soak** and **goal** and **tail**.

food foot

Finally, a word of advice ...
Remember that **book** sounds different from **boot**.
You don't want to mix up your **foot** with your **food**.

Brick was scared of the **dark**.

ar

1. Sound out the word and then blend the sounds together.

dark

2. Trace the dotted grapheme with your finger.

dark

3. Write the grapheme.

ar ....

Other words with the **ar** sound:

car

part

bark

or

1. Sound out the word and then blend the sounds together.

torch

2. Trace the dotted grapheme with your finger.

t o r ch

3. Write the grapheme.

or

Other words with the or sound:

born

fork

sport

Oz used Bogart as a **torch**.

Brick learned to **surf**.

ur

1. Sound out the word and then blend the sounds together.

surf

2. Trace the dotted grapheme with your finger.

3. Write the grapheme.

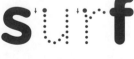

Other words with the **ur** sound:

burn

curl

fur

er

1) Sound out the word and then blend the sounds together.

herd

2) Trace the dotted grapheme with your finger.

herd

3) Write the grapheme.

er ....

Other words with the **er** sound:

her

germ

fern

Grit loved his **herd** of sheep.

Armie really
needed a
shower.

ow

1 Sound out
the word and
then blend the
sounds together.

shower

2 Trace the dotted
grapheme with
your finger.

sher

3 Write the
grapheme.

ow ....

Other words
with the
ow sound:

cow

down

now

oi

1) Sound out the word and then blend the sounds together.

soil

2) Trace the dotted grapheme with your finger.

3) Write the grapheme.

Other words with the oi sound:

coin

join

point

Bearnice waited for something to grow from the **soil**.

SUSHI

Another round of salmon maki for the table, please!

Complete these words using the sushi stickers. When you're done, blend the sounds to read each word.

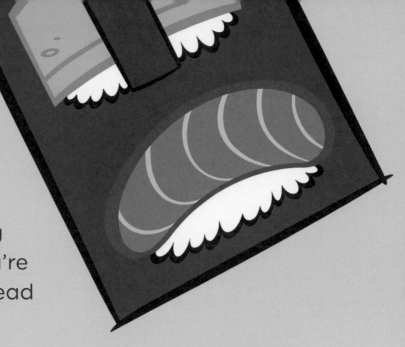

p | Add sticker here. | k

b | Add sticker here. | l

Turn to page 170 for stickers.

t

Add sticker here.
n

f
Add sticker here.

k

p

Add sticker here.

er

th
Add sticker here.

n

SPOT THE ALIENS

Oh no ... There's been an alien invasion in the backyard!
Alien words don't mean anything. Can you find the real words?

Read each word carefully to help you decide if it is real or alien.
Put a **sunflower sticker** under the real words and an **alien sticker**
under the alien words.

Remember, you can add sound buttons
to help you read the words.

coin

Add sticker here.

ver

Add sticker here.

Turn to pages 170 and 171 for stickers.

germ

shoin

Add
sticker
here.

Add
sticker
here.

chorb

town

Add
sticker
here.

Add
sticker
here.

car

cark

Add
sticker
here.

Add
sticker
here.

BEACH DAY

Bogart is taking some time to relax!

Can you spot anything buried in the sand around him? Use stickers to complete the words.

1 c **Add sticker here.** d

2 c **Add sticker here.** l

3 s t **Add sticker here.**

Turn to page 171 for stickers.

126

4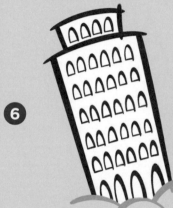

Add sticker here. l

5 c Add sticker here. n

6  t Add sticker here. e r

7  Add sticker here. l

8  f l o w Add sticker here.

Hey, you there! Slow **down**! Hold your horses!
At this rate, you'll be teaching this book how to read!

a
dark
burp

a corn surf

a bark frown

You've read **dark**, **torch**, **herd**, and **shower** and **soil**.
But what about **bark** and **mermaid** and **boil**?
There's **corn** and **burp** and **thorn** and **frown**.
There's **surf** and **germ** and **porch** and **gown**.

Yang has a **fear** of spiders.

ear

1. Sound out the word and then blend the sounds together.

fear

2. Trace the dotted grapheme with your finger.

f **ear**

3. Write the grapheme.

Other words with the **ear** sound:

ear

hear

year

air

1. Sound out the word and then blend the sounds together.

hair

2. Trace the dotted grapheme with your finger.

h**air**

3. Write the grapheme.

air ....

Other words with the **air** sound:

pair

chair

fair

Bearnice hated brushing her **hair**.

Oz felt **tired** after a hard day of playing.

ire

1. Sound out the word and then blend the sounds together.

tired

2. Trace the dotted grapheme with your finger.

3. Write the grapheme.

ire ....

Other words with the **ire** sound:

wire

fire

hire

ure

1. Sound out the word and then blend the sounds together.

cure

2. Trace the dotted grapheme with your finger.

c ure

3. Write the grapheme.

ure ....

Other words with the **ure** sound:

sure

pure

lure

Don't worry, Bearnice! Armie has the **cure**!

YIN AND YANG'S BIRTHDAY

It's the thought that counts! Help Yin and Yang unwrap their strange collection of birthday presents.

Circle the word that matches each gift.

1

chair
dear

2

tire
wire

3

air
hair

4

fire
lair

5

cure
earring

6

armchair
vampire

TOASTING MARSHMALLOWS

Bogart can't wait to toast even more marshmallows! Complete these words using the delicious-looking marshmallow stickers. When you're done, blend the sounds to read each word.

Add sticker here.

air

Add sticker here.

ear

Turn to page 174 for stickers.

s

Add sticker here.

f

Add sticker here.

h

Add sticker here.

ch

Add sticker here.

n

Add sticker here.

DETECTIVE MYSTERY

When you read a text, there are some words you need to recognize by sight because you can't sound them out.

These are called high-frequency words because they come up in texts often.

1 Trace and write out these high-frequency words.

we _____

they _____

you _____

are _____

was _____

2 Read these phrases.

we cook

they run

you swim in the pool

you **are** a good dog

I **was** wet from the rain

Stax needs to find the words in the purple boxes. Help him solve the mystery by drawing lines to connect the matching words.

we	they	you	are	was

was hill they

hat pool

pat are we

not

you

SCRAPBOOK!

Bearnice is scrapbooking!
Help her match the captions to the pictures.

Read each phrase and stick the matching picture sticker above it.

we had fun

Add sticker here.

she was glad

Add sticker here.

I will miss you

Turn to pages 174 and 175 for stickers.

Add
sticker
here.

they are tired

Add
sticker
here.

**they jump
in mud**

you are my pal

Add
sticker
here.

**he looks at
the stars**

Add
sticker
here.

**they are on top
of the hill**

Would you look at that! This book's almost done!
But your reading adventures have just begun ...

a
hair
chair

There was **fear** and **hair**, and **tired** and **cure**.
Now there's **near** and **fair**, and **wire** and **pure**.
Chair, **pair**, and **air**, and **clear**, **dear**, and **ear**.
Let's ramp it up and see what we find here ...

Allure, endure,
And **caricature**.
Admire, inspire,
And **firefly** and **dire**.
Hairstyle, **stairwell**,
Airport, and **fairground**.
Nearest, **dearest**,
Clearance, and **fearless**.

And when you're **fearless**,
the sky is no limit!

Pages 22–23
Your answers might include:
sat, sap, tap, tan, pat, pan, nap

Pages 24–25
Your answers might include:
sit, sip, sin, tip, tin, pit, pip, pin, nit, nip

Pages 26–27
All words are sound buttoned as follows:
sip nap pan tan tap sap sat

Pages 28–29
Real words: sit, sip, tap, nit, pit
Alien words: tas, san, nas

Pages 40–41
Your answers might include:
sock, top, pot, pop, not, nod, mop, mock, dot, dog, dock

Pages 42–43
1 dog **2** pan **3** pen **4** pig
5 mop **6** net **7** sock **8** sack

Pages 44–45
Your answers might include:
set, ten, pet, pen, peg, peck, net, neck, met, men, den, deck, get

Pages 48–49

the cat

I nap

I am sick

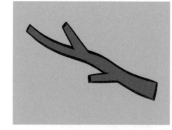
a stick

the pig

a snack

the sad dog

to the top

Pages 62–63
Your answers might include:
sun, suck, put, pun, puff, nut, mud, mug, muck, dug, run, rug, hut, hug, huff, but, bun, bug, buck, fun, luck

Pages 64–65
All words are sound buttoned as follows:
fill fog miss duck tell bill bun sniff

Pages 66–67
1 bed **2** sun **3** bat **4** bell
5 rat **6** kiss **7** hot **8** cliff

Pages 68–69
1 bag **2** hat **3** cog
4 bug **5** doll **6** bus

Pages 78–79
box, jam (**or** yam), wig (**or** jig), yes, zip, web, six

Pages 80–81
1 wig **2** fox **3** jam **4** web
5 six **6** box **7** zipper

Pages 84–85

she is sad

my bed

her pen

he is glad

my bag is big

she is in the box

her hat is big

he sat on the hill

Pages 94–95

thick (**or** chick **or** quick), quick (**or** chick **or** thick), chin (**or** shin **or** thin), jazz, song (**or** sock), shock

Pages 96–97

1 ship **2** ring **3** fish
4 moth **5** shell **6** chess

Pages 98–99

Real words: quit, thing, shop, such
Alien words: wung, chiss, kizz

Pages 108–109

night, need, look (**or** leek), queen, wait, moon (**or** moan **or** main), coat

Pages 110–111

1 boat **2** book **3** bee **4** boot
5 light **6** train **7** seed **8** wool

Pages 112–113

1 coat **2** right **3** tool **4** nail
5 sheep **6** wood **7** snail

Pages 122–123

park (**or** pork), boil, turn (**or** torn **or** town), fork, power, thorn

Pages 124–125

Real words: coin, germ, town, car
Alien words: ver, shoin, chorb, cark

Pages 126–127

1 card **2** curl **3** star **4** owl
5 corn **6** tower **7** oil **8** flower

Pages 134–135

1 chair **2** wire **3** hair **4** fire
5 earring **6** armchair

Pages 136–137

fair (**or** hair), year (**or** fear **or** hear), sure (**or** sear), fire (**or** fear **or** fair), hear (**or** hair **or** hire), chair, near

Pages 140–141

we had fun

she was glad

I will miss you

they are tired

they jump in mud

you are my pal

he looks at the stars

they are on top of the hill

CONCOCTED BY MRS WORDSMITH'S CREATIVE TEAM

Pedagogy Lead
Eleni Savva

Writers
Tatiana Barnes
Amelia Mehra

Academic Advisor
Emma Madden

Associate Creative Director
Lady San Pedro

Designers
Jess Macadam
James Webb

Lead Designer
James Sales

Producer
Leon Welters

Artists
Brett Coulson
Giovanni D'Alessandro Jr.
Phil Mamuyac
Aghnia Mardiyah
Nicolò Mereu
Maggie Mikan
Daniel J. Permutt

With characters by
Craig Kellman

concoct
v. to make something by mixing ingredients

No animals were harmed in the making of these illustrations.

Project Managers
Senior Editor Helen Murray
Senior US Editor Kayla Dugger
Senior Designer Anna Formanek

Senior Production Editor Jennifer Murray
Senior Production Controller Lloyd Robertson
Publishing Director Mark Searle

First American Edition, 2022
Published in the United States by DK Publishing
1745 Broadway, 20th Floor, New York, NY 10019

Printed and bound in China

For the curious
www.dk.com

mrswordsmith.com

MIX
Paper | Supporting
responsible forestry
FSC™ C018179

This book was made with
Forest Stewardship Council™
certified paper—one small
step in DK's commitment to
a sustainable future.

The building blocks of reading

READ TO LEARN

LEARN TO READ

Phonemic Awareness → Phonics → Fluency → Vocabulary → Reading Comprehension

Readiculous App
App Store & Google Play

Word Tag App
App Store & Google Play

OUR JOB IS TO INCREASE YOUR CHILD'S READING AGE

This book adheres to the science of reading. Our research-backed learning helps children progress through phonemic awareness, phonics, fluency, vocabulary, and reading comprehension.

Stick **before** letters at the beginning of the word
and **after** letters at the end.

Before   After

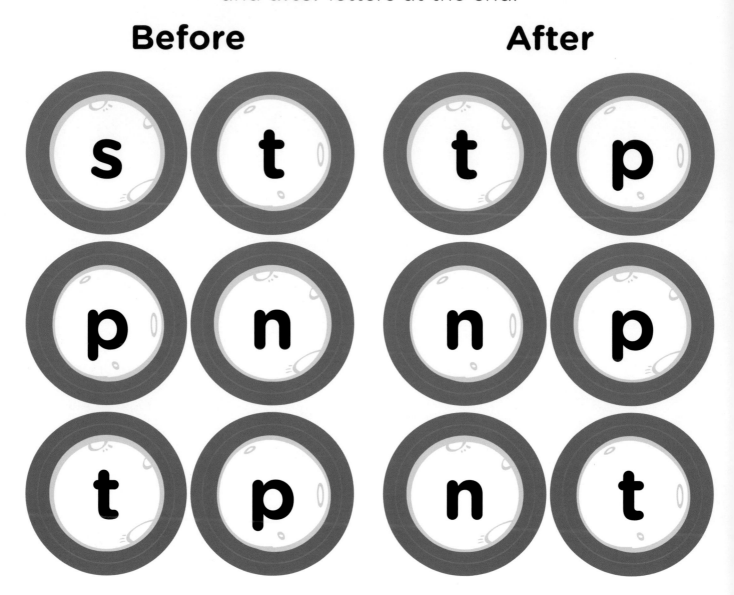

Stick **before** letters at the beginning of the word
and **after** letters at the end.

Before   After

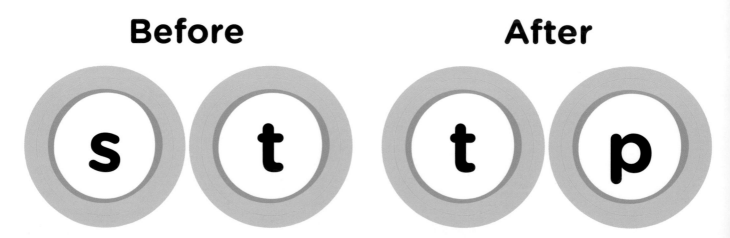

Before   After

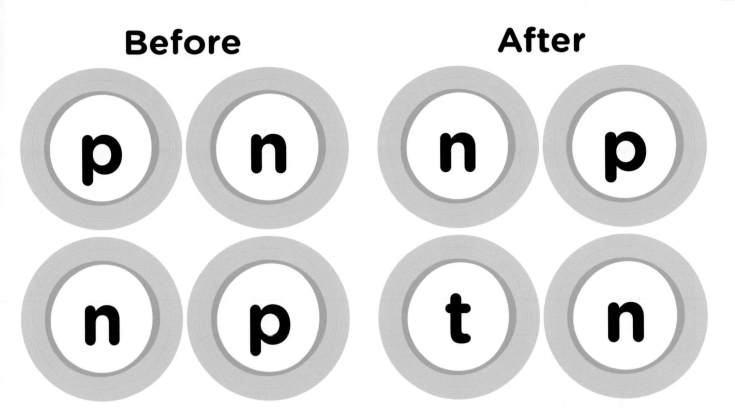

STICKERS > P.28–29

Stick **before** letters at the beginning of the word
and **after** letters at the end.

Before   **After**

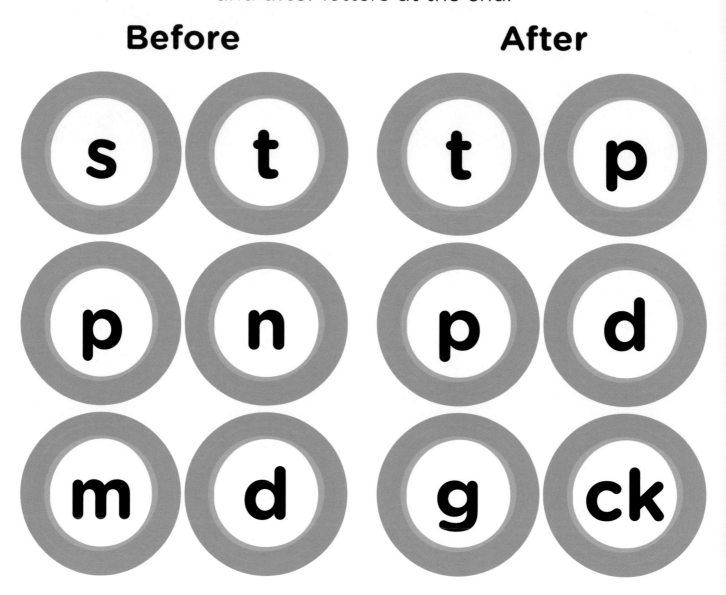

STICKERS > P.44–45

Stick **before** letters at the beginning of the word
and **after** letters at the end.

Before   **After**

Before

After

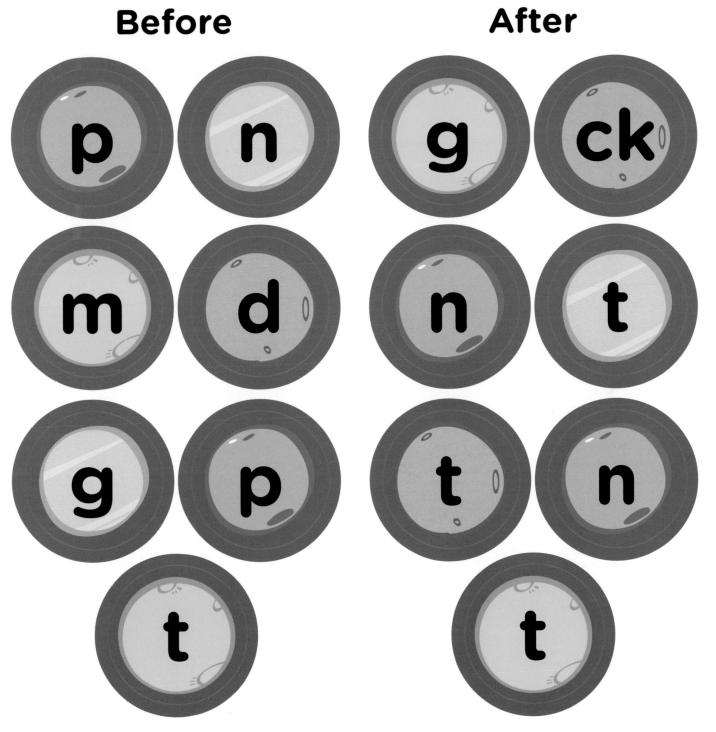

STICKERS > P.48

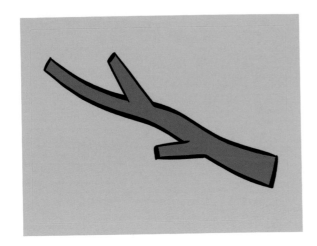

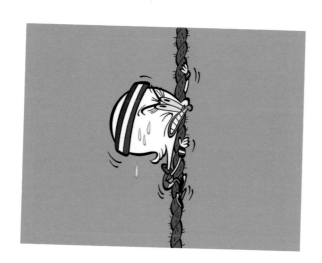

BONUS STICKERS

Stick **before** letters at the beginning of the word
and **after** letters at the end.

Before

After

s

p

t

p

n

m

n

d

d

r

g

ck

h

b

d

ff

f

l

t

n

STICKERS > P.62-63

Stick **before** letters at the beginning of the word
and **after** letters at the end.

Before

b

p

b

After

n

d

t

STICKERS > P.68-69

ll

u

g

b

h

c

BONUS STICKERS

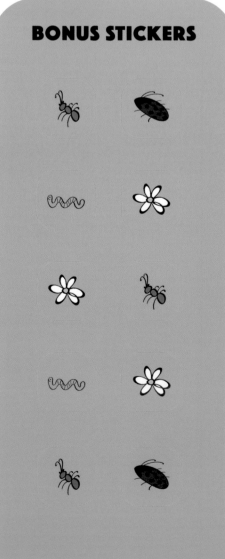

STICKERS > P.78-79

j

x

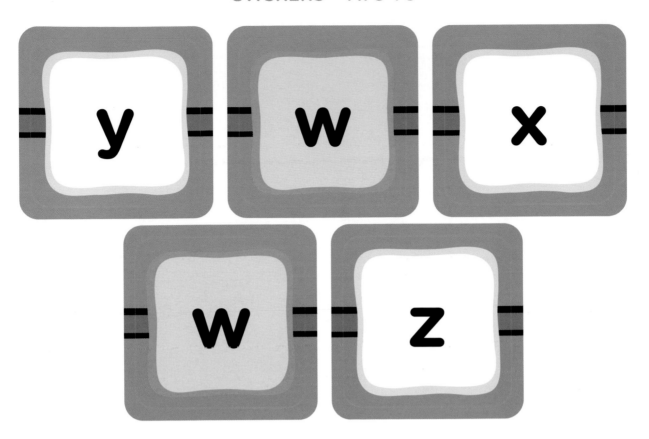

STICKERS > P.84

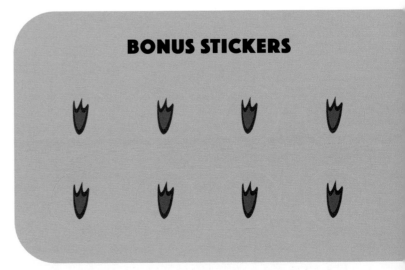

BONUS STICKERS

STICKERS > P.85

STICKERS > P.94–95

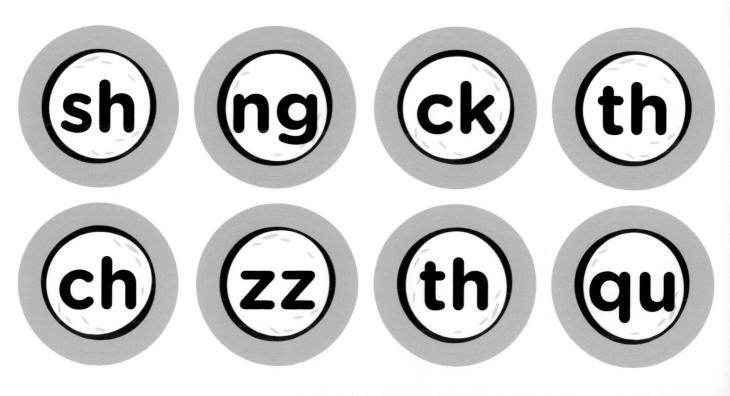

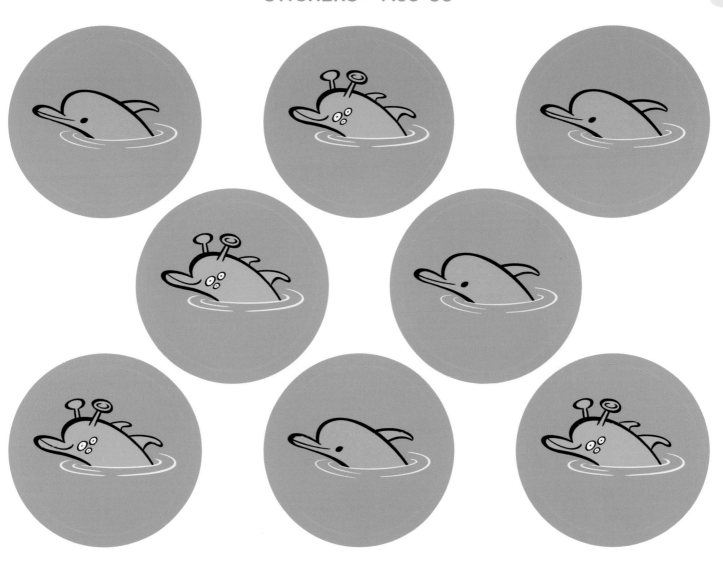

BONUS STICKERS

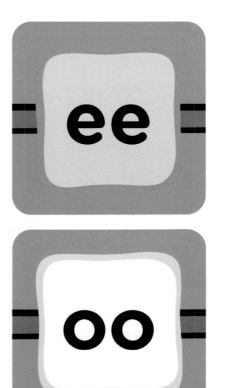

STICKERS > P.108–109

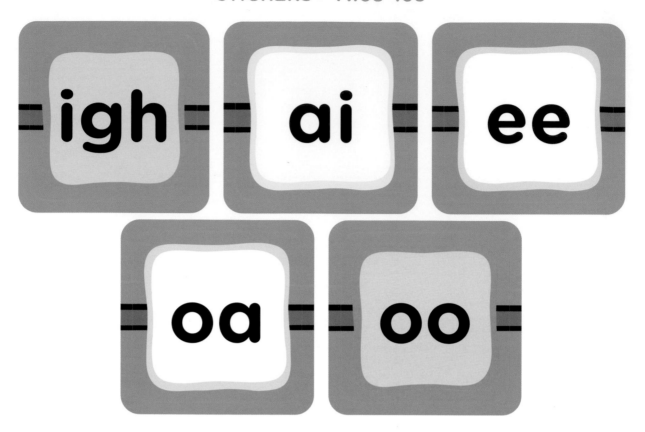

STICKERS > P.122–123

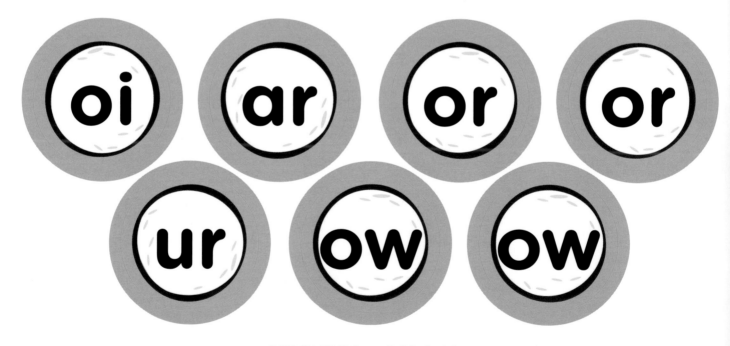

STICKERS > P.124–125

STICKERS > P.126–127

o w	u r	a r
o r	e r	o i
a r	o w	

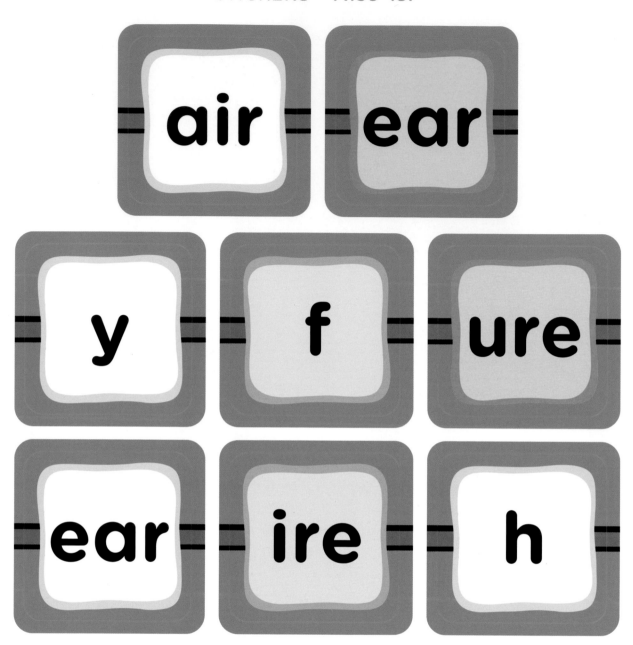

STICKERS > P.140

BONUS STICKERS